I G O R
SIKORSKY

Father of the Helicopter

Steven Otfinoski

Withdrawn

ROURKE ENTERPRISES,INC.
VERO BEACH, FLORIDA 32964

A Blackbirch Graphics Book.

Library of Congress Cataloging-in Publication Data

Otfinoski, Steven.
   Igor Sikorsky / by Steven Otfinoski.
      p.   cm. — (Masters of invention)
   Includes bibliographic references.
   Includes index.
   Summary: A biography of the aircraft designer and manufacturer who pioneered in multi-engine airplanes, helicopters, and flying boats.
   ISBN 0-86592-100-8
   1. Sikorsky, Igor Ivan, 1889–1972—Juvenile literature.
2. Aeronautical engineers—Biography—Juvenile literature.
[1. Sikorsky, Igor Ivan, 1889–1972. 2. Aeronautical engineers.]
I. Title. II. Series.
TL540.S54O84   1993
629.13'0092—dc20
[B]   93-2822
                                                            CIP
                                                            AC

CONTENTS

CHAPTER ONE

RUSSIAN DAYS

*Thousands turned out to cheer the local boy who
had brought such honor to their city.*

*I*gor Ivanovich
Sikorsky was born into a relatively well-off
Russian family on May 25, 1889, in Kiev, the
capital city of Ukraine (formally a republic of
the USSR, now an independent country). He
was the youngest of five children. His father,
I. A. Sikorsky, was nationally known for his
pioneering work in the field of psychology,
which deals with the mind and behavior. Dr.
Sikorsky lived for work. Besides maintaining a
private practice as a psychologist and teaching
regularly at the local university, he managed to
write almost a hundred books. Igor's mother
was also dynamic. She was a medical-school
graduate at a time when few Russian women
even worked outside the home. She was also
a gifted pianist.

**Opposite: Igor Sikorsky's courage and vision changed our
understanding of aviation forever. His innovations and
achievements have affected people all over the world.**

A Dream of Flight

Young Igor did not at first seem to possess the same capacity for hard work that his parents had. He was a fragile child. Because of this, he was forced to spend much of his time at home. There, he read adventure books and daydreamed a lot. One of his favorite books was *Clipper of the Clouds* by French science-fiction writer Jules Verne. In his novel, Verne imagined a flying machine that could go in any direction. Igor could think of nothing else but this fabulous machine. People had already conquered the skies in hot-air balloons and very light airships known as dirigibles. Their flying ability, however, was very limited. But unlike dirigibles, Verne's flying machine was a heavier-than-air craft. Many people at the turn of the century thought that Verne's vehicle was pure science fiction and would stay that way. But young Igor was not one of them.

Igor developed a keen curiosity about science and had a talent for bringing scientific ideas to practical use. He soon progressed from building wooden toys to making simple electric batteries and small motors. When he was only 12, Igor made a working model of a flying machine that was powered by rubber bands. He called his machine a "helicopter," a word already in use. *Helicopter* comes from the Greek words *heliko*, meaning spiral, and

At 12 years old, Igor made his first working model of a flying machine. He powered it with rubber bands.

pteron, meaning wing. Igor believed that spiral wings would allow a pilot to move in any direction he or she wanted. By 13, he was building a motorcycle driven by steam. He was also building homemade bombs, much to his neighbors' concern. But it was the helicopter that continued to be Igor's main interest.

In 1903, Igor entered the St. Petersburg Naval Academy. That same year, two brothers, Orville and Wilbur Wright, of the United States, took a flimsy, heavier-than-air flying machine to the sand dunes of Kitty Hawk, North Carolina. Their flying machine, carrying one of them, left the ground for a few seconds. In those precious moments, the Wright Brothers had proven that a heavier-than-air vehicle could indeed fly as no balloon ever could. The age of modern aviation was born.

From Helicopters to Airplanes

The Wright brothers' achievement inspired young Igor. In 1906, at age 17, he left the Naval Academy to become an engineer and build his own flying machine. At that time,

Igor designed and built his first helicopter around 1906, when he was only 17. Although it never left the ground, this early model set the stage for Igor's later successes.

Paris was the center of the new field of flight in Europe. Igor went to Paris and enrolled in an aeronautics school. The "school" consisted of students standing around and watching airplane builders as they worked in a hangar. Their passion for flying inspired Igor. In only four months he returned to Kiev and designed and built his first helicopter. It never left the ground. A second attempt, with a more powerful engine, was also a flop. Igor realized that the helicopter was much more complicated than an ordinary airship. It would take a lot more study and experiment. He put his dream on hold, and as he later wrote, he temporarily "entered the fixed-wing business."

His first successful flying machine was called the S-2 (S for "Sikorsky"). It was very primitive by today's standards. The airship had no instruments, and bicycle wheels served as landing gear. But amazingly, it flew—200 yards at an altitude of 2 to 4 feet. The first flight lasted less than a minute. It ended when the S-2 crashed into a swamp. Igor rebuilt the damaged plane. And the next time, it reached the unheard of altitude of 100 feet. Then it, too, crashed, through the thin ice of a pond. Igor, who was piloting the plane, nearly drowned. But he managed to crawl out of the wreckage just in time.

Throughout 1911, Igor continued to work on improving his aircraft. He eventually flew a half hour in the air at a peak altitude of 1,000 feet. His achievements were beginning to attract attention outside Kiev. At age 22, he was presented to the Russian king, Czar Nicholas II. In 1912, Igor's three-seater biplane, the S-6A, won the gold medal at the Moscow Aircraft Exhibition. Igor was offered a position as designer and chief engineer at a new aircraft plant. It was owned by the Russian Baltic Railroad Car Factory, which was better known for making railway and motor cars than airplanes. The Baltic Company agreed to let Igor build one experimental aircraft each year, along with his other duties. Igor no longer had to rely on the loans of his father and older sister Olga to finance his dreams.

Igor's ambitions continued to grow. In 1913, he designed and built a four-and-a-half ton aircraft. It was the world's first plane with four engines. It had a 92-foot wingspan and a pilot's cabin with two seats and an instrument panel. Igor named the huge aircraft the *Grand*—French for "large." Few believed that the *Grand* would ever leave the ground. But it did, carrying eight people aloft for nearly two hours. The *Grand* set one long-distance record after another. Finally, it was accidently destroyed when an engine from another plane fell on it from above.

Igor's next project was an even bigger plane. This time he named it the *Ilia*

In 1913, Igor created the *Grand*—the world's first four-engine plane, weighing four-and-a-half tons.

Mourometz, after a 10th-century hero of Kiev. It could carry 16 people. In June 1913, Igor and some friends rode the *Ilia* from St. Petersburg to Kiev—a distance of 800 miles. While in the air, they sat down to the first full meal ever eaten on board a flying aircraft. The arrival of the airplane in Kiev was a glorious event. Thousands turned out to cheer the local boy who had brought such honor to their city.

The *Ilia Mourometz*, one of Igor's early creations (1913), was large enough to carry 16 people. It was later used as a bomber during World War I.

Planes for War

In 1914, Russia joined the fight in Europe against Germany and the Austro-Hungarian and Ottoman empires in World War I. Russia's allies included France, England, and later, the United States. Flying machines, once an amusement, were suddenly weapons of destruction. The Russian army ordered Igor to build 10 of his 4-engine airships to be used as fighter planes and bombers. During the war, Igor built 75 bombers for the army. In about 400 bombing raids only one plane was ever lost. This was an almost unbelievable record.

But the Russian army fought mostly on the ground, where it was no match for the German fighting force. Tens of thousands of Russian soldiers died on the battlefield. The war was unpopular with the Russian people. And it increased their dissatisfaction with the czar's government. In 1917, in the midst of the war, a revolution took place. New leaders seized control of the country. They killed the czar, his family, and thousands of Russian nobles and other well-to-do people. Igor, who was from a respectable, middle-class family, was not trusted by the new leaders. The government secretly destroyed his planes, arrested his friends, and shut down his aircraft factory. Fearing that he, too, would be arrested, Igor decided to leave Russia and seek a new life abroad. In February 1918, he fled from St. Petersburg to the port of Murmansk on the Arctic Sea. There, he caught a British steamer for England. He would never lay eyes on his native land again.

CHAPTER TWO

AMERICAN DREAMS

Igor wasn't about to give up.

When Igor first set foot in England, it, along with the rest of Europe, was still in the midst of war. Optimistic about building fighting aircraft for the Allies, Igor traveled to France to offer his services to the French army. There, he was hired to build a huge bomber for the French. The plane was nearly finished when, without warning, the war ended with Germany's defeat.

Hard Times

With peace, the need to build new and better airplanes quickly faded. The Europeans were not interested in Igor's plans for commercial

Immigrants at the turn of the century catch their first glimpse of the Statue of Liberty. Igor was one of many people who came to America during the early 1900s to seek his fortune.

aircraft. Flying as a means of transportation still seemed like a dream to most people. The 30-year-old Igor turned his sights to the United States, where he thought his dreams might be taken more seriously. He got a visa (permission to go to another country) and boarded a steamship bound for New York City.

On March 30, 1919, Igor Sikorsky arrived in New York knowing just a few words of English and carrying less than $600 in his pocket. His reputation as an aviation pioneer had not traveled with him, however. To the customs officer on duty at Ellis Island, he was just another foreigner who couldn't speak English. Moreover, Igor found the same lack of interest in airplanes in America that he had found in Europe. He tried to arouse investors' interests, but he had little success. He met with aviation experts in Washington, D.C., but nothing came of that either. Igor finally landed a job in the Engineering Division of the Army Air Service, building a three-motor bomber. Then the army dropped the project.

With no prospects for work in aviation, Igor tried to get any kind of job just to survive. He found nothing. He spent his days in his tiny six-dollar-a-day room or at the New York Public Library, sketching plans of airships that it seemed would never be built. He lived on a steady diet of Boston baked beans and coffee, a twenty-cent meal that included free bread and butter. Then, when his money was nearly gone, he found work as a math instructor at the New York Russia Collegiate Institute. Like Igor, these students were also from Russia. At the institute, he met a pretty Russian lady who taught at a children's school. Her name was Elizabeth Semion. They fell in love and were married in 1924.

The First Factory

Besides teaching math, Igor began lecturing on aviation and astronomy. The Russians in his classes were impressed by his passion for airplanes. They listened eagerly as he talked about building a 4-motor, 50-passenger airplane. Together, they pooled $800. With this small sum, Igor and his supporters founded the Sikorsky Aero Engineering Company. One friend, Victor Utgoff, had a chicken farm on nearby Long Island. He invited Igor to set up his factory there. The "factory" was, by any standards, a humble one. The workshop and office were housed in a large chicken coop. The parts came from local junkyards. The hangar was the great outdoors. Working conditions, as one of Igor's friends recalled, were complicated by the chickens who ate the rivets off the ground. "During the week," said Nick Glad, "we worked on the airplane outdoors, and the chickens ran around under our feet.

On the weekend, we would kill and eat the chickens and take the rivets from their crops [throats] to use the following week."

Among Igor's most generous stockholders (people who own part of a company) was the Russian composer Sergey Rachmaninoff. Rachmaninoff bought $5,000 worth of stock in the company. The money was spent moving Igor's finished airplane to a real hangar on Long Island's Roosevelt Field.

On May 4, 1924, Igor was ready to give the S-29A (A for "America") its first test flight. The company had so little money that it couldn't afford a barrel of gasoline for fuel. It had to drag in a few cans from a nearby filling station.

Igor sat at the controls. Eight co-workers had come aboard as passengers. The plane lifted off, circled the field at 100 feet, barely missed hitting some telegraph wires, and finally landed on a golf course. The plane then ran into a ravine and partially turned over. Fortunately, no one was injured. As Igor inspected the damaged plane, he overheard one of his mechanics whisper, "This is the end."

Igor wasn't about to give up. He had worked five years to get this plane built, and he was going to see it fly. He told his crew to dismantle the plane to rescue the parts. Then he tried to figure out where he would get the money to rebuild it. He decided to turn to his friends one last time. He assembled 50 of them together in his office and locked the door. He said he wouldn't open the door until they raised, among themselves, another $2,000 for a new engine.

Success at Last

Igor's friends gave him the money, and on September 25, the S-29A was ready to take to the skies once more. The plane climbed to 1,000 feet, circled for 10 minutes, and made a clean landing. Igor's faith in his plane had been justified. Now all he needed was money to pay back all of his loyal supporters and to continue development.

The Sikorsky company received its first job offer—to carry two grand pianos from New York to Washington, D.C. One of the pianos was going to future first lady, Mrs. Herbert Hoover. The publicity Igor received from the important piano job was helpful and he soon got other work.

Each year through the 1920s, Igor designed and built a new and better airplane. In 1925, he built a two-seater observation plane. The next year he designed and built a two-motor transport plane, the S-35, for the famous French flyer Captain René Fonck. Fonck's ambition was to be the first aviator to fly by himself from New York to Paris across the Atlantic Ocean. The first attempt met with a

In 1925, Igor's company received its first commission—to transport two grand pianos from New York City to Washington, D.C. Here, one of the pianos is played just after it was delivered.

disaster on the runway that killed two men. But by the spring of 1927, Fonck and Igor were ready to try again—this time with a new plane. News arrived that airmail pilot Charles A. Lindbergh had landed in Paris in his plane, *The Spirit of St. Louis.* Overnight, Lindbergh became an international celebrity.

Lindbergh's success helped Sikorsky. His solo flight captured the public's imagination, and the world renewed its interest in air flight. By 1929, business was booming at Igor's plane factory. Igor needed more factory space for production, so he moved his operation to Stratford, Connecticut, on Long Island Sound. He wanted to be near the water to continue development of his latest creation, a new kind of aircraft that was revolutionizing flight.

FLYING BOATS

Igor was...very much the European gentleman.

Seaplanes, which can take off and land on water, were developed before Igor built his. Igor's, however, were much better than the others. His S-38 was a twin-engine aircraft with a hull-shaped fuselage (the plane's central structure for crew, passengers, and cargo) that could hold enough fuel for long distance flights. The plane had two short lower wings that carried two floats for water landings and takeoffs. The S-38 would certainly win no beauty contests. One critic called it "a collection of airplane parts flying in formation." But it also earned a reputation as "the world's safest airplane." At a top speed of 130 miles per hour, it was also one of the fastest.

The S-38 caught the interest of the U.S. Navy and Pan American Airways, one of the first and most successful companies of American commercial airlines. Pan Am bought a number of S-38's and used them for new passenger flights they were making to Latin America. Pan Am's top-level consultant was famous aviator Charles Lindbergh. Lindbergh visited the Sikorsky factory and he and Igor became lifelong friends. On the surface they were very different people. Lindbergh was tall, handsome, and All-American. Igor was of medium height, balding, and very much the European gentleman. But they shared two things—a passion for aviation and a respect for each other.

Lindbergh flew Igor's first flying boat to the Panama Canal to inaugurate airmail service to this American-occupied zone. The S-38's were so successful that other countries wanted them. Chile ordered one plane, and Igor himself flew it part of the 7,000 miles from the United States to Santiago, Chile's capital.

The success of the S-38 had allowed Igor to make the move to Connecticut. There, he designed and built a more powerful flying boat, the S-40, which had four motors. It was flown to Washington, D.C., and christened the *American Clipper* by First Lady, Mrs. Herbert Hoover. Lindbergh flew the *American Clipper* to Colombia with Igor aboard as a passenger. During the long flight, Igor started sketching a new design for a flying boat that could cross the Atlantic Ocean. On reaching Kingston, Jamaica, Lindbergh examined Igor's sketch over dinner. Then the two men began to work together to improve the design. "We turned the menu upside down and drew on it," recalled Igor later, "and before we finished dinner, Lindbergh and I knew what our next aircraft should look like."

Igor and Charles Lindbergh began working together on Igor's Pan American Airways project in the 1930s. Their meeting sparked a friendship that lasted a lifetime.

Igor checks in with the pilot of his new Amphibian S-43. The plane was intended to service the Hawaiian Islands.

The End of an Era

The last of the Sikorsky flying boats was the S-44A. The original model—the one after which the S-44A was patterned—was called the *Excalibur.* The plane flew nonstop from New York to Rome, Italy, a distance of 4,600 miles. Yet, for all their achievements, flying boats were quickly becoming obsolete.

New airports around the world made long nonstop flights unnecessary. Newer land planes were sleek and more efficient. Flying boats had served their purpose, but a new day of aviation was dawning.

As the 1930s ended, Igor Sikorsky turned his attention from conventional aircraft to his old dream—the one he had first had years before as a youth in Russia. That dream was the helicopter.

CHAPTER FOUR

BIRTH OF
THE HELICOPTER

*"It is like a dream to feel the machine lift you
gently up in the air...."*

*A*n aircraft that could rise vertically and move in any direction had fascinated people for centuries. The Chinese had designed a children's toy that operated on the principle of direct-lift flight around 300 A.D. Leonardo da Vinci, the gifted Italian artist and scientist of the Renaissance, sketched a workable helicopter in 1483. Leonardo's copter flew under the power of a screwlike wing made of starched linen. Two hundred years later, two Frenchmen built the first workable helicopter in Europe that actually flew. Its two rotors (large horizontal propellers that spin to give a helicopter lift and propulsion) were made of feathers.

Throughout the 19th century, inventors struggled to get a full-size helicopter off the ground. The engines and motors they used for power were either too weak or heavy to get the helicopters up in the air. By the beginning of the 20th century, experimental helicopters had lifted off the ground and gone into free flight. A twin-rotor helicopter designed by the German Henrich Focke actually stayed aloft for nearly an hour and a half. But these early helicopters were not reliable. They wobbled in the air and were extremely difficult to control. By the 1930s, a practical helicopter still remained a dream.

Igor's Nightmare

Despite his early failures with designs, Igor began thinking again about helicopters in the mid-1930s. United Aircraft Corporation, which had bought Igor's company in 1934, gave him $30,000 to build an experimental helicopter. Igor decided that one reason helicopters had failed to fly was that they had two overhead rotors. He believed one rotor, if powerful enough, could achieve free flight.

By 1939, Igor's experimental craft was ready to be tested. He called it the VS-300. For many people on and off the company lot, it was "The Ugly Duckling," or "Igor's Nightmare." Ugly it certainly was. The aircraft was

Igor made his first successfully controlled vertical helicopter flight on May 20, 1940. This primitive version of the helicopter reached an elevation of 30 feet.

a crude skeleton of steel with an open pilot's seat in front. There were two control sticks—one for climbing and descending and one for controlling the pitch and roll. The three-blade rotor above helped the helicopter to rise. A tiny, single-blade rotor in the rear kept the balance. The motor had 75 horsepower. "If that thing ever flies," said one of Igor's top engineers, "I have never been, am not, and never will be an engineer."

The first flight of the VS-300 was hardly memorable. Igor, as always, was his own test pilot. The helicopter shook violently as it rose several inches off the ground for about 10 seconds. It couldn't have risen much higher, in any event. The aircraft was secured to the ground with cables and weights to prevent it from turning over and to keep it close to the ground for careful observation. With each test, however, performance improved. Gradually the weights were reduced, and the cables were loosened. Eventually the precautions were removed altogether.

The first free-flight test took place on May 13, 1940. Five days later, the public came to watch. Igor flew his helicopter backward, sideways, and up and down. The spectators were astonished. After the display, Lester Morris, the Connecticut commissioner of aeronautics, presented Igor with Connecticut Helicopter Pilot License Number 1. When

United Aircraft Corporation president, Eugene Wilson, asked the inventor Igor why he had flown the helicopter in every direction but forward, the designer smiled and replied, "That is one of the minor engineering problems we have not yet solved!"

With time and much painstaking work, Igor did solve his helicopter design problems and worked out many other minor "bugs." Under Igor's tender care, "The Ugly Duckling" blossomed into a graceful swan of the skies.

An Oddball Pilot

The 51-year-old designer was as delighted with his invention as a child is with a new toy. "During my thirty years of activities in aviation, I have never been in the air in a machine that was as pleasant to fly as this light helicopter," Igor wrote in his autobiography, *The Story of the Winged-S.* "It is like a dream to feel the machine lift you gently up in the air, float smoothly over one spot for indefinite periods, move up or down under good control, as well as move not only forward or backward but in any direction."

One day, Igor took off from the factory yard in his helicopter and disappeared. His co-workers began to grow worried when the "old man" didn't return from his latest test flight. A small group rushed to a nearby rock

On May 6, 1941, Igor broke a stationary flight record in his VS-300. He remained aloft within a 30 foot circle for 1 hour, 32 minutes, 25 seconds.

quarry. They wondered if Igor had crash-landed in the quarry's depths. Suddenly, to their great relief, the VS-300 rose out of the hole in the ground. When Igor landed, he explained, "I thought it would be pleasant to fly down into the quarry and take a look around."

Soon he was flying his helicopter all over Stratford, frightening the cows in their pastures and causing surprised citizens to scratch their heads and smile.

Igor's flying uniform was hardly standard pilot's gear. He wore street clothes, an overcoat to avoid a chill, white tennis shoes for comfort, and his faithful floppy hat, which he lovingly referred to as "a good luck charm and crash helmet." He didn't dress like this merely because he was an oddball. Igor had a point to make. He was convinced that the helicopter would be the first aircraft used by the ordinary person. He envisioned people commuting to work each morning in private little helicopters, free of the stresses of highway traffic. It was a novel idea whose time, unfortunately, has not yet come.

With the VS-300 perfected, Igor wasted no time in building a bigger and better helicopter. The XR-4 (*X* for experimental and *R* for rotary wing) was twice as big and powerful as the VS-300. The army was impressed and tested it under every possible condition. To publicize his latest helicopter, Igor flew it from Connecticut to the army's Wright Field in Dayton, Ohio. The 16-hour, 10-minute flight covered 761 miles and set a record. Thousands of curious onlookers got their first glimpse of this strange, hovering flying machine. Igor startled motorists by occasionally pulling down alongside them to ask for directions. When a mechanic in Buffalo, New York, told his father about the strange contraption, the older man gravely replied, "Son, I want you to give up aviation. When you start seeing things like that, it's time to make a change!"

Helicopters in War and Peace

The army was deeply impressed by Igor's helicopter. When the United States entered World War II in 1941, his helicopters went to the battlefront, rescuing downed fliers behind enemy lines. Igor's company turned out more than 200 helicopters during the war years.

In 1943, Sikorsky moved its plant to an old foundry in Bridgeport, Connecticut. There, he developed the S-51, the first commercial helicopter. By 1949, the SS-55, a 10-passenger helicopter, was making the first scheduled passenger runs in a helicopter.

When the Korean War broke out in 1950, Sikorsky helicopters were called in. They observed enemy positions and strengths and carried troops and much-needed supplies to areas where no regular airplane could go. The helicopter was rescuing so many American soldiers behind enemy lines that it earned the nickname "Guardian Angel."

In the 1950s, lighter and more powerful helicopters were built. Helicopters began to

Igor never let a failure pass without learning from it. Here, he inspects a Sikorsky S-51 helicopter that crash-landed in Bridgeport, Connecticut, 1944.

be used for many important everyday purposes, including transportation and construction work, crop-dusting in agriculture, aerial observation of traffic flow for television and radio audiences, and rescue missions in natural disasters. Nearly every astronaut who has gone into space has been recovered upon splashdown by a helicopter.

On November 1, 1959, Igor and three companions pioneered as passengers aboard a platform attached to the Sikorsky S-60 crane helicopter. The passengers endured an elevation of 1,500 feet and a speed of 71 knots.

Since Igor's first flight, helicopters have proved to be not only unique, but essential aircraft. They have the ability to take off and land in the smallest of spaces, hover for hours in midair, and to fly safely at much lower altitudes and slower speeds than airplanes. The helicopter has lived up to Igor Sikorsky's claim of being "a universal method of transportation which is truly more independent of conditions on the ground than any other vehicle known, even the pack mule."

CHAPTER FIVE

THE
PHILOSOPHER

*His spirit still soars today—in his helicopters
he made with such care and love.*

*I*gor Sikorsky retired
as engineering manager of Sikorsky Aircraft at
age 68 in July 1957. He spent the remaining
15 years of his life, however, as a very active
man. Igor became an engineering consultant
for the company and he kiddingly referred to
himself as "resident genius." Everyday he
drove to the office in his Volkswagen beetle.
There, he usually sported a baggy tweed suit
and a baseball cap. It is a measure of the man
that he wouldn't park in front stalls with other
top executives. Instead, he parked in the back
of the lot with the regular employees.

Igor never stopped working hard. He
continued to design new and more efficient

To many, Igor represented the true "courtly gentleman." He was a man of passion, intellect, and kindness.

helicopters. Perhaps his finest contribution in retirement was the Skycrane, a flying crane helicopter. It was used to lift and move large oil and mineral cargo.

A Man of Many Interests

Igor had more time, however, to devote to his many interests, such as astronomy, ancient history, and volcanoes. His modest house in the Connecticut countryside had a small observatory in the backyard. He traveled the globe to investigate some of the world's most famous volcanoes. He once flew a helicopter into the crater of Paricutín, a volcano in Mexico, just so he could take a picture of it.

Perhaps Igor's greatest passion, aside from aviation, was religion and philosophy. As a devout member of the Russian Orthodox Church, he wrote several books about his faith. In *The Message of the Lord's Prayer* (1942), Igor studies and thinks about this famous Christian prayer to more fully explore its spiritual meaning. *The Invisible Encounter* (1947) deals with mysticism and the conflict between materialism and spirituality in the modern world. In this book, Igor calls the twentieth century "one of the darkest periods of human history." He claims that the spiritual renewal of modern civilization is the only hope to rescue it from destruction.

Igor received the nation's highest science medal, awarded by the National Academy of Sciences, from President Lyndon Johnson on February 13, 1968.

Although a man of science, Igor was doubtful about science's ability to solve the world's problems. "Science is neutral," he wrote. "That is the trouble with science. It is strictly neutral to good and evil....Science is something of which mankind must be careful."

A "Perfect Gentleman"

A deeply thoughtful man, Igor was also kind and generous. For all his years spent in America, he remained a courtly European gentleman until his dying day. He treated

Igor and two small friends enjoy the sights of the New York World's Fair in 1964.

everyone—whether a corporation president or a lowly employee—with the same respect and graciousness. He had "beautiful Old World manners," recalled one plant worker. "When he met someone, he would always click his heels and bow. If it was a woman, he would also kiss her hand." Before leaving his office for the day, he would always shake hands warmly with his longtime secretary and say, "Thank you, Katusha, you have been a great help to me."

In his last years, Igor was forced to rely more and more on the help of others. He developed an eye disease and gradually lost his sight. One night in 1970 he walked outside his home to see the constellations. "He came back into the house, visibly depressed," Sergei, his eldest son, recalled, "and said with sadness, 'I can no longer see the stars.'"

The Legend Lives On

Two years earlier, Igor had been seriously ill for several weeks. But despite all his suffering, he never lost his sense of humor. "I had scheduled my departure from this world in

Three astronauts pay a visit of appreciation to Igor in 1972. The three men were retrieved by a Sikorsky helicopter after they had splashed down in the ocean on one of their missions.

1968," he told a friend. "But someone has apparently canceled my passage. Maybe I'll reschedule it for the coming year."

There was no cancellation on October 26, 1972, when Igor quietly died of a heart attack at home. He was 84 years old and his mind was still as active as ever. The wake took place at Saint Nicholas Russian Orthodox Church, the church he had helped build years earlier.

The effect that his death had on one former Sikorsky employee, Don Richardson, echoed that of many who knew him: "It hit me then, that we had lost the last of the true aviation pioneers....It was the end of an era."

Nevertheless, the life and legend of Igor Sikorsky live on in the helicopters that he dreamed about as a boy and designed and built as a man. And, even if he had never made a single helicopter, Igor would still be remembered for his first four-motor airplane, his flying boats, and his many other remarkable aviation achievements.

A man of deep faith and moral conviction, as well as a great scientist, Igor Sikorsky was truly a man for all seasons. Perhaps Ann Lindbergh, the wife of Igor's most celebrated friend, said it best: "He can soar out with the mystics and come straight back to the practical, to daily life and people." His spirit still soars today—in the helicopters he made with such care and love.

GLOSSARY

altitude Height.

aviation Science of flight; development and operation of heavier-than-air craft.

biplane Airplane with two sets of wings, one above the other.

dirigible Airship that can be directed or steered.

fuselage Central body of an airplane that contains crew, passengers, cargo, and fuel.

hanger A shelter for aircraft.

helicopter Aircraft that rises vertically and moves in any direction.

observatory A building equipped with a large telescope for astronomical research.

rivet Metal bolt or pin with a head, used as a fastener.

rotor Large horizontal propeller.

seaplane Aircraft that can take off and land on water.

FOR FURTHER READING

Barrett, Norman S. *Helicopters.* New York: Franklin Watts, 1989.

Rosenbaum, Robert. *Aviators.* New York: Facts on File, 1992.

Stacey, Tom. *Airplanes: The Lure of Flight.* San Diego, CA: Lucent Books, 1990.

White, D. *Helicopters.* Vero Beach, FL: Rourke Publishing, 1989.

INDEX

Photo Credits

Cover: Bettmann; p. 4: UPI/Bettmann; p. 11: The Bettmann Archive; p. 12: The Bettmann Archive; p. 15: Library of Congress; p. 20: The Bettmann Archive; p. 24: AP/Wide World Photos; p. 25: UPI/Bettmann; p. 28–29: UPI/Bettmann; p. 32: UPI/Bettmann; p. 35: AP/Wide World Photos; p. 36: AP/Wide World Photos; p. 39: AP/Wide World Photos; p. 41: UPI/Bettmann; p. 42: AP/Wide World Photos; p. 43: AP/Wide World Photos.

Illustrations by Dick Smolinski.